The

GOSPEL

cántaro
publications

A PUBLISHING IMPRINT OF THE CÁNTARO INSTITUTE

Steven R. Martins

The

GOSPEL

Foundation Series
Vol. 1

cántaro
publications

cantaroinstitute.org

The Gospel, Foundations, Vol. I
Published by Cántaro Publications, a publishing imprint of
the Cántaro Institute, Jordan Station, Ontario, Canada

For volume pricing, please contact
info@cantaroinstitute.org

Library & Archives Canada
ISBN: 978-1-990771-25-5

Printed in the United States of America

TABLE OF CONTENTS

Chapter One

AN UNFOLDING NARRATIVE

WHAT IS THE GOSPEL? The word "gospel" is a translation from the Greek *euaggelion* (εὐαγγέλιον), which means "good news". Whose good news? *God*'s good news. And to whom is this news "good" for? That would be us, you and me. This news is good for all of God's creation.

In the Greek text of the New Testament, the word "gospel" is used 77 times. The first time we find this word (if we do not include the titles of the four New Testament gospels) is in Matthew 4:23, which states:

> And [Jesus] went throughout all Galilee, teaching in their synagogues and proclaiming the gospel of the

kingdom and healing every disease and every afflic-
tion among the people.

And while it is written that this gospel was first
preached to the Jews, it is later noted that this gospel would be preached to the Gentiles. As the apostle Peter testified in Acts 15:7:

> …"Brothers, you know that in the early days God
> made a choice among you, that by my mouth the
> Gentiles should hear the word of the gospel and be-
> lieve."

What is this gospel? How should we answer
that question when we are asked by our peers?
While the gospel can certainly be communicated
with simplicity (*and it very well ought to be*), it is
also much more comprehensive and expansive than
what most Christians today believe it to be. Some
say the gospel has to do with the forgiveness of sin,
others also include the eternal life we are promised
in the Son, that being Jesus Christ, and there are
various other "gospel" components that are empha-
sized depending on who you speak with, such as restored peace between man and God, the promise of
paradise, the escape from the judgment of God, etc.

None of these can be denied as forming part of the "good news", as a matter of fact, they are irremovable from the gospel, but they are often communicated in piecemeal fashion, and not as part of a *systematic whole*. The Christian intellectual Francis Schaeffer was right in his assessment when he said that "the basic problem [in recent years] of Christians... is that they have seen things in bits and pieces instead of totals."[1] Such is the case with the gospel, it is often communicated in bits and pieces, and when the attempt is made to communicate it in its totality, we witness another failure that serves as proof of the anemic state of the modern church, the *truncation* of the gospel.

Again we ask, What is the gospel? This good news, this gospel, is articulated by the whole of Scripture, both Old and New Testaments, in the form of Creation-Fall-Redemption. In order for there to be "good" news (Redemption), there ought to be "bad" news that precedes it (Fall), and in order for there to be "bad" news, there must be some ideal state which precedes the bad and the good

1.   Francis Schaeffer, *A Christian Manifesto*, (Westchester, IL.: Crossway Books, 1981), 17.

(Creation). When we use the term "news", we pre-suppose that some event has occurred. In other words, we can begin by asking, What was the state of things *originally*? Then, What happened that *altered* the state of things? And lastly, What was done to *remedy* that alteration? The answers to these questions are what is communicated to us in the biblical form, or scheme, of Creation-Fall-Redemption. And this book seeks to answer those questions in an attempt to communicate the *total* gospel.

Chapter Two

CREATION

*"In the beginning, God created
the heavens and the earth."*
— Genesis 1:1

WHAT WAS THE STATE of things *originally*? When we use the phrase "the state of things", we mean "the state of creation." In Genesis 1:1 we read that, "In the beginning, God created the heavens and the earth." Every living creature, every created entity, everything from the seen and the unseen — and this includes the 95% of the cosmos that we have yet to discover and which lies beyond our observational range — was created by God. Outside of God Himself, who is uncreated, there is nothing that exists that was not created. As Nehemiah 9:6 reads:

You are the Lord, you alone. You have made heaven,
the heaven of heavens, with all their host, the earth
and all that is on it, the seas and all that is in them;
and you preserve all of them; and the host of heaven
worships you.

As God reveals in the Scriptures, God is good,
and nothing of evil or deceit is found in Him
(e.g., Ps. 34:8; 145:9; Jas. 1:17). Thus, when He
created the cosmos, including that which was within man's range of reach and that which was not,
He created all things "good." In fact, Genesis 1 uses
the word "good" seven times (Gen. 1:4, 10, 12, 18,
21, 25, 26-31), and this evaluation of creation's
goodness was not from human judgment, but from
the Creator Himself. The Hebrew word used for
"good" here is *tov*, and the term "very good" is *hennah tov*. While both *tov* (בוֹט) and *hennah tov* are
not explicitly defined but rather assumed, the word
"good" as used in the creation account is in reference to the qualitative sense of functionality. God
called everything good because everything fulfilled
the function for which He designed them. And giv-
en that the standard by which we measure "goodness" is God Himself, as the Sovereign Creator, if

He judges that something is good (or not good), then it is just that.

Creation was "good" the moment God created it, and prior to the fall of our first parents, the historic Adam and Eve, everything was "good". This included everything that was, and everything that was meant to be as mankind dedicated himself to fulfilling the creational mandate. This means that whatever functioned within the creational law-spheres, which can be listed as the arithmetical, the spatial, the kinematic, the physical, the biotic, the psychical, the analytical, the historical, lingual, social, economic, aesthetic, juridical, ethical, and pistical (or faith), from the a-normative (those laws that cannot be violated, e.g., laws of nature) to the normative (those laws that can be violated, e.g., morals), it was to all evidence the goodness of God's creation.[1]

The Creational Mandate

What was the creational mandate? The creational

---

1. For more on the creational law-spheres, see Steven R. Martins, *Towards a Christian Understanding: The Pursuit of a Christian Philosophy* (Jordan Station, ON.: Cantaro Publications, 2022).

mandate is what God called man to do, and this includes both the man and the woman. We find this in Genesis 1:28:

> And God blessed them. And God said to them, "Be fruitful and multiply and fill the earth and subdue it, and have dominion over the fish of the sea and over the birds of the heavens and over every living thing that moves on the earth."

If you understood the central significance and abiding validity of the word "dominion" in this text, as it relates to the purpose and function of man, you would be surprised how many today have neglected or dismissed this part of the text. But it is precisely because this text is so often overlooked that much of the church has an anemic or truncated understanding of the gospel. What does it actually mean to "subdue" and "have dominion"? Herman Bavinck, Christian theologian of the late nineteenth and early twentieth century, had this to say:

> Gen. 1:26 teaches us that God had a purpose in creating man in His image: namely that man should *have dominion...* If now we comprehend the force

14

of this subduing (dominion) under the term of *culture*... we can say that *culture* in its broadest sense is the purpose for which God created man after his image.[2]

To put it more simply, man's creational mandate was to cultivate God's creation into a godly civilization. And for this reason, this *creational* mandate is also referred to by theologians as the *cultural* mandate, because whatever man does, as he interacts with creation, he creates and cultivates "culture". An acre of woodlands, for example, is God's creation, but if man were to transform that acre into a neighbourhood, that would be culture. Or a tomato would be God's creation, but if man were to turn that tomato into a sauce for a pizza, that would be culture.

The Image of God

How is the creation and cultivation of culture made possible? Why is it that the creational mandate is

2. Herman Bavinck, "The Origin, Essence and Purpose of Man", in *Selected Shorter Works of Herman Bavinck*, ed., John Hendryx (West Linn, OR.: Monergism Books, 2015), loc. 469.

given only to mankind? For the reason cited by Bavinck: because only mankind is created in the image of God. No other creature, no other created entity, shares this privilege, this honour, of being created in the *imago Dei*. As we read in Genesis 1:26:

> Then God said, "Let us make man in our image, after our likeness. And let them have dominion over the fish of the sea and over the birds of the heavens and over the livestock and over all the earth and over every creeping thing that creeps on the earth."

To be created in the image of God means to be like God as much as a creature (created being) possibly can, *without violating* the Creator-creation distinction. In terms of character, all that is found to be "good" in man finds its root source in the character and being of God. This includes his ability to love, to be kind, to be gentle, to be merciful, etc. We might think of the fruits of the Spirit in Galatians 5:22-23. In terms of intelligence, this includes man's ability to form and understand concepts, to recognize patterns, to plan and innovate, to solve problems and make decisions, to retain information, to develop, use and understand communicative and non-communicative languages, etc. If we want to be more precise in our understanding of man's uniqueness and distinction from the rest of creation as being created in the image of God, we could use the fifteen creational law-spheres, as articulated by the Christian philosopher Herman Dooyeweerd, as a reference. Based on those fifteen law-spheres (see Figure 1), what differentiates the created human race from *other* living things is our ability to function within the normative law-spheres, from the analytical, to the historical, the lingual, the social, the economic, the aesthetic, the juridical, the ethical, and the pistical (or faith). While animals, on the other hand, are restricted to the a-normative law-spheres, from the arithmetical, to the spatial, to the kinematic, the physical, the biotic, and the psychical. Man certainly operates within these law-spheres, but man is not *restricted* to them. What about plant life? Plant life does not factor into the conversation because it is a different kind of "life" as described by Scripture. Both mankind and beasts have the breath of life, the Hebrew *nephesh* (שפנ); plant life, however, is not identified as having *nephesh*.

The fact that mankind is created in the image of God is presupposed, stated, and implied throughout all of Scripture. In Old Testament law, for example, we find the affirmation of mankind's inherent dignity as being based on the fact that he bears God's image. And this too we also find in the teachings of the New Testament (e.g., the Sermon on the Mount). Never at any point, in all of the Scriptures, is the image of God dismissed or dishonoured in any of its prescriptive passages (Scriptural passages that instruct and/or direct us as to how we ought to live). And though we might question whether the image of God is still left in man given the decadence and depravity of our age, *nowhere in Scripture does it state that the image of God has been erased in man.* In light of all that God has created, from galaxies to black holes, to protons and electrons, to quarks and preons, the entirety of Scripture leaves us with no doubt that though mankind may appear as nothing significant in this vast tapestry of creation, mankind is nonetheless the crown jewel. If man were to be the wax, and God the seal, we are the impression left by the seal upon the wax. And what a privilege to be the only created thing to bear such an impression. No wonder the Psalmist wrote:

> When I look at your heavens, the work of your fingers,
>> the moon and the stars, which you have
>> set in place,
> what is man that you are mindful of him,
>> and the son of man that you care for him?
> Yet you made him a little lower than the heavenly beings
>> and crowned him with glory and honor.
> You have given him dominion over the works of your hands;
>> you have put all things under his feet...
> (Ps. 8:3-6).

The Threefold Relationship of Man

If all of creation was declared to be good according to its Creator, according to our God, then that means that man's threefold relationship was also good, or to put it another way, it functioned as it was designed to function. Man has a threefold relationship that cannot be divorced from his creature-ly existence. As the Christian philosopher Danie

F.M. Strauss writes:

> The human self is nothing in itself, that is, it does
> not exist separately from the three central relation-
> ships in which God had placed human beings. First
> of all human beings stand in relation to God, then
> in relation to their neighbours, and lastly in relation
> to the totality of created temporal reality.[3]

To lay it out simply: First, man has a relationship with God. Man was created *by* God and
for God, and being created after the divine image
meant that he could have a relationship with God
that far transcends what other creatures could possibly experience. We do not read in Genesis 3 that
God walked and talked with the animals,[4] nor did
He do this with *non*-living things, everything below mankind (if we regard man as the crown jewel)

3.   D.F.M. Strauss, *Being Human in God's World* (Jor-
     dan Station, ON.: Paideia Press, 2020), 66-67.

4.   His address to the serpent is not to be considered a
     form of "fellowship" or "dialogue", it is not compa-
     rable to God's interactions with man, but rather it
     is to be regarded as a pronouncement of judgment
     upon both the creature used by the adversary, and
     upon the adversary himself, Satan.

lacks the capability and functionality of such fellowship with the Creator. However, we are told, and quite explicitly in various ways, that man has a relationship with God, one unique from that of the rest of creation. Genesis 3:8 informs us that God regularly walked with Adam and Eve in the garden; personal fellowship between God and man was a norm. There was peace, *Shalom* (מוֹלְשׁ) between God and man.

Second, man also has a relationship with fellow man. In the beginning, the first created human beings were Adam and Eve. Adam was the head, Eve was the helper, both occupied different roles, but both were equal in their inherent dignity and value, and both were expected to fulfill the creational mandate. As the first man and woman, and in the giving of the woman to man, God instituted the first marriage (Gen. 2:18-25), and from this marriage would come the entirety of the human race.[5]

---

5. For more on the multiplication of the human race and responses to commonly made challenges to the biblical genealogy, see AiG, "Who Was Cain's Wife?", *Answers In Genesis*. Accessed Nov. 8, 2022, https://answersingenesis.org/bible-characters/cain/who-was-cains-wife/ and any references provided therein.

How was man to function in relation to his fellow man? The Old Testament law explained it, but Jesus summarized it in the form of the second greatest commandment, which is "Love your neighbor as yourself" (Matt. 22:39). And this commandment was fulfilled so long as man kept the greatest commandment above this one, "Love the Lord your God with all your heart and with all your soul and with all your mind" (Matt. 22:37).

Third, man has a relationship with creation. I had mentioned earlier that man's creational mandate was to cultivate God's creation into a godly civilization, that is precisely what man's relationship to creation was and is to look like. How was that to be done? By fulfilling the threefold calling of man, which was to serve as God's (i) prophet, (ii) priest, and (iii) designated king. As God's prophet, he was to interpret creation according to God's revelation. As God's priest, he was to consecrate creation unto God through his every creational interaction. And as God's designated king, he was to rule and govern subject to the rule and governance of God. Man was God's steward. For this reason, God prepared a special garden (Eden) in which the man and the woman could begin their stewardship duties, and this was meant to be extended to all the earth as they multiplied and filled it (Gen. 1:28; 2:15).[6]

All of creation was declared to be good, and this meant that everything functioned as it was designed to function.

6. See *La Fuente: Iberoamerican Journal for Christian Worldview*, Vol. 2, No. 1, "The Purpose and Call of Man" (Jordan Station, ON.: Cantaro Publications, 2022).

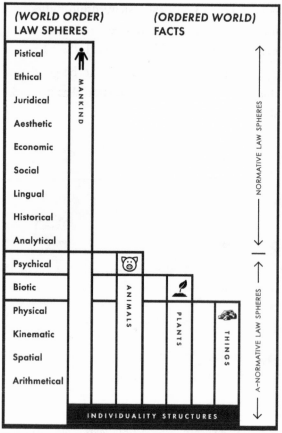

Figure 1: *The Creational Law-Spheres and what it means to be human.*

Chapter Three

FALL

And the LORD God commanded the man,
"You are free to eat from any tree in the garden;
but you must not eat from the tree of
the knowledge of good and evil,
for when you eat from it
you will certainly die."
– Genesis 2:16-17

WHAT HAPPENED THAT *altered* the state of things? Evidently, the world we live in now does not match the depiction we read of in Genesis 1 and 2. Something happened, and whatever happened, it was cosmically significant. This is what *altered* the state of things:

When God placed our first parents, the historical Adam and Eve, in the Garden of Eden,[1] they

---

1. See Terry Mortenson, *Searching for Adam: Genesis*

were given the liberty to eat any fruit or produce in the Garden. Genesis 2:16 records God saying "You are free to eat from any tree in the garden". But that freedom came with a condition. That one condition was that man was not to eat from "the tree of knowledge of good and evil" (v. 17). What made this tree so special? Unlike the tree of life, which was placed in the middle of the Garden alongside the tree of knowledge (Gen. 2:9), there was actually *nothing special* about this tree. On the contrary, it was just as natural as any of the other trees in the garden. The tree of life allowed man to "live forever" (Gen. 3:22), which also served as a prophetic symbol for the Christ who would be later revealed in the grand narrative (Rev. 2:7; 22:2, 14), but the tree of knowledge held no special (or supernatural) properties itself. There is a reason why this is so, and why it cannot be to the contrary. This tree had to be just as natural as all the other trees in order that, by obeying God in relation to this one tree, man might know how to obey God in relation to every other creational aspect. It could be said that man's obedi-

---

& the Truth about Man's Origin (Green Forest, AR.: Masterbooks, 2016).

ence to God's commands would be determined by his obedience in relation to this one natural tree. If he could obey God in this one simple task, which was to not eat from the tree, then man could obey God in his every interaction with creation. Does this then mean that there was only a single commandment that man was to obey? In one sense, yes, and in another sense, no. Yes, in the sense that it was a commandment that was communicated verbally, clearly, and explicitly by God, and we read of no other *verbal* commandment in chapters 1, 2, and 3 of Genesis. However, the answer is also No, because by creating man after His image, God had placed His law in the heart of man. And we see this law later revealed in rest of the Pentateuch (Genesis to Deuteronomy), and further expounded on in the rest of the Old Testament through the prophets, and in the New Testament through the teachings of Jesus and the apostles. The late Christian theologian Cornelius Van Til explains this latter point of God's law residing in man's heart:

> As a creature of God, man had to live in accordance with the law of God, that is, in accordance with the ordinances that God had placed in his creation. This

law was for the most part *not verbally transmitted* to man but was created in his being. Man would act in accord with his own true nature only if he would obey the law of God and, vice versa, if he would live in accord with his own nature, he would obey the law of God.[2]

What would happen if our first parents were to eat from the forbidden tree? If only it remained an "if". The fact of the matter is that they did eat from the forbidden tree. This is the fall (Gen. 3). When Adam and Eve succumbed to the temptation presented to them by the possessed serpent (Gen. 3:4), they brought about "the fall" of mankind and creation.

The Meaning of Disobedience

Before addressing "the fall" in its comprehensiveness, we must first understand what this act of disobedience meant: When Adam and Eve ate from the forbidden tree, they did so in pursuit of a complete and total independence from God. In other

---

2. Cornelius Van Til, *Christian Apologetics*, Second edition, ed. William Edgar (Phillipsburg, NJ.: P&R Publishing, 2003), 42 (emphasis mine).

words, they sought to be like God in a way that was improper for a creature, to be like God in a way that blurred the Creator-creation distinction. It was not enough to be created in God's image, they desired to be *equal* to God, to be *gods*. As Van Til writes: "When man fell, it was therefore an attempt to do *without God* in every respect." How so? By substituting the Creator with creation, "[m]an sought his ideals of truth, goodness, and beauty somewhere beyond God, either directly within himself or indirectly within the universe about him."[3] Prior to this act of disobedience, man knew what was "good" because his source of knowledge was God, and because he was created in the image of God, he knew what goodness was. His knowledge, just like his being, is derivative of God. Thus man did not know evil. But by eating from the forbidden tree, he gained the knowledge of evil *by committing evil.* And it would become apparent to Adam and Eve that the tree of knowledge granted them no special power, it was a tree like all the rest, and in place of gaining something they lost something of great value, their innocence. Thus the

---

3. Ibid., 42 (emphasis mine).

lie of the serpent was exposed. They were not made equal to God, but in their pursuit of such independence, they disobeyed God. They committed "sin" in their hearts by eating from the forbidden tree. What is sin? The Hebrew word for sin is *hhatah* (האטח), which translated literally means "to miss the mark." Throughout the Scriptures, the word "sin" is described as to mean transgression (or violation) of the law of God, and rebellion against God Himself. In terms of the transgression of the law, 1 John 3:4 states generally that:

> Everyone who makes a practice of sinning also practices lawlessness; sin is lawlessness.

And in terms of rebellion against God, Deuteronomy 9:7 states in reference to the Hebrews:

> Remember and do not forget how you provoked the Lord your God to wrath in the wilderness. From the day you came out of the land of Egypt until you came to this place, you have been rebellious against the Lord.

Perhaps the most illustrative passage of Scripture is Psalm 51, written by King David, the second king of Israel (1 Sam. 16:1-13) and credited as being a man after God's own heart (Acts 13:22). This Psalm illustrates the meaning of sin in its heartfelt, poetic expression, written after his grave sin against God through his adultery with Bathsheba and the murder of her husband Uriah (2 Sam. 11-12). In Palm 51:5 he writes "in sin did my mother conceive me", which meant that since the moment he was conceived he was sinful, the effect of the fall. His whole person required a "purging," he was essentially defiled, needing to be cleansed. Put another way, David was saying that his being was broken, unclean, foolish, weak, false, guilty, and that whatever his person did wrongly against another was ultimately done against God. As his Psalm explains: (i) sin is judged by God (Ps. 51:4), (ii) it cuts one off from the presence of God (v. 11), and (iii) it silences all praise (v. 15). All of Scripture testifies of this truth, for it reveals a God who is just, holy, and righteous.

Prior to the fall, there was no presence of sin in God's creation. Everything was created "good." Man had peace with God, with his fellow man (in Adam's case, with his wife Eve), and with creation. There was an unbroken fellowship between God, the man, and the woman. But everything changed when sin entered the world. And for one who only knew what was good, you can imagine the effect that sin had upon the heart of man. It is like the poison of a lethal snake bite, once you are bitten, it begins to corrupt and compromise the whole, such is sin to the nature and being of man. And not only is man affected, but his every relationship, as well as everything that was placed under him, everything of which he was to subdue and over which he was to exercise dominion. The late nineteenth to mid-twentieth century theologian Geerhardus Vos explains the effects of sin upon the nature and being of man:

> By falling away from something to which he was wholly disposed, which constitutes his proper and highest destiny, man [was] changed in the deepest depths of his being; [1] a radical reversal [would] take place within him... So, if original righteousness falls away, [2] unrighteousness replaces it as the natural state.[4]

---

4.   Geerhardus Vos, *Reformed Dogmatics*, Vol. 2: Anthropology, trans. and ed. Richard B. Gaffin, Jr. (Bellingham, WA.: Lexham Press, 2014), 14.

The Effects of Sin upon the Threefold Relationship of Man

This "radical reversal" inevitably meant man's alienation and separation from God; no longer could man enjoy the unbroken fellowship he once had with God. What was holy was made unholy, and what is *un*holy cannot have fellowship with what is holy, for it offends the holy by being antithetical to it. As the prophet Isaiah wrote:

> But your iniquities have made a separation
>   between you and your God,
> and your sins have hidden his face from you
>   so that he does not hear (Isa. 59:2).

Adam and Eve once walked in the Garden with God, now such an experience became foreign to mankind because their sin no longer made that possible. Where once man was *willfully subject* to God, in his sin, mankind became *hostile* toward God (Rom. 8:7). Where once there was *peace* between God and man, now man wages *war* against the King of all creation. How can we understand this? By understanding the nature of sin. The first sin, the *original* sin, would become the root of all sin. And what was that sin? It was to be radically *autonomous*, independent from God, to be a "law" (Gr. *nomos*) unto "oneself" (Gr. *autos*). And such rebellion has been described as "cosmic treason". It was the late theologian R.C. Sproul who said:

> Every sin, no matter how seemingly insignificant, is an act of rebellion against the sovereign God who reigns and rules over us and as such is an act of treason against the cosmic King.[5]

If someone were to violate the law today, a violation that would fall under the criminal code for example, how would we refer to that person? As a criminal. If a convicted murderer were to be walking freely up and down the streets, society would be in an uproar. Why? Firstly, because justice demands that his or her crime be answered for. And secondly, because he or she poses a danger to the general public. In the same way, our acts of rebellion against God's law are to be seen for what they are, not as mere misdemeanors, but as felonies deserving of punishment. We, who threaten to do

5. R.C. Sproul, "Cosmic Treason", *Ligonier*. Accessed Nov. 10, 2022, https://www.ligonier.org/learn/articles/cosmic-treason/.

violence against the holiness, glory, and righteous-ness of God, stand three times condemned; firstly, because of our inherited sinful nature (which can be understood as spiritual death and depravity) (Ps. 51:5), secondly, because of our imputed sin (that is to say, we have been credited with the sin of our first parents) (Rom. 5:13), and thirdly, because of our daily personal sins.

Let me address the first: If we are spiritually dead, then we cannot have fellowship with the God of life, nor can we do anything spiritually good, for how can a corpse do anything? Instead, our depra-vation ensures our separation from God.

In regard to the second: Because the law of God has been revealed in Scripture, we are held responsible for the sins of our forefathers, chiefly that of Adam. Consider what God says in Exodus 34:7b, that He:

> ...will by no means clear the guilty, visiting the iniq-uity of the fathers on the children and the children's children, to the third and the fourth generation.

Those familiar with the judgment history of Old Testament Israel will know this to be a fact.

Consider also what Paul has to say about Adam's relation to our account of sin:

> Therefore, just as sin came into the world through one man [Adam], and death through sin, and so death spread to all men because all sinned… (Rom. 5:12).

In regard to the third: We cannot deny that we *personally* commit our own transgressions against the law of God, and for that we are also held responsible.

If only that was all that had to be said, but man's relationship with God is not the only one affected. The violence that results from man's sin extends to his other two relationships as well, that with fellow man, and that with creation.

In regard to his relationship with fellow man, we read in Gen. 3:12 that man turned against his wife, and that this was but a glimpse of a conflict that would continue between them over the course of history. This conflict between husband and wife is mentioned in Genesis 3:16b, which says: "Your desire shall be contrary to your husband, but he shall rule over you." But we also see this conflict

FALL

mentioned earlier as between their descendants in
general (3:15a): "I will put enmity between you [the
adversary] and the woman, and between your offspring and her offspring." In the marital instance,
God says that the woman would desire to supplant
God's creational order by desiring headship, but
that the man would instead rule over her (3:16).
Hebrew commentator Franz Delitzsch provides us
with insight as to the original state of things and
what sin brought about:

> Created for the man, the woman was made subor-
> dinate to him from the very first; but the supremacy
> of the man was not intended to become a despotic
> rule, crushing the woman into a slave... the original
> revelation, that of a rule on the one hand, and sub-
> ordination on the other [were to] have their roots in
> mutual esteem and love.[6]

Husband and wife were to live together in perfect harmony, sin, however, ruptured that harmony.

The more general instance, however, would become all the more evidenced to our first parents in

6. Carl Friedrich Keil and Franz Delitzsch, *Commen-
   tary on the Old Testament*, Vol. 1 (Peabody, MA.:
   Hendrickson, 1996), 64-65.

the murder of their son Abel by his brother Cain (Gen. 4:8). This is the first recorded event of human bloodshed, and it would not be the last. Delitzsch has this to say in relation to Cain's act of murder and the conflict God had said would manifest in Gen. 3:15a:

> In [Cain] the seed of the woman had already become the seed of the serpent; and in his deed the real nature of the wicked one, as "a murderer from the beginning," had come openly to light: so that already there had sprung up that contrast of two distinct seeds within the human race, which runs through the entire history of humanity.[7]

This mention of two contrasting seeds will be expanded on in the next chapter, for now, it is sufficient to say that sin has deeply affected man's relationship with fellow man.

What about the third relationship, that with creation? Prior to the fall, man's relationship to creation as its cultivator and developer expressed itself in the form of joyful work. Whether it was in tending the Garden (Gen. 2:15), naming the animals

---

7.   Ibid., 71.

(Gen. 2:18-20), cultivating creation into a godly civilization (Gen. 1:28), or any other potentiality that would arise as a result of man's advancement and flourishment, work was a relative joy and it was done unto the glory of God. Popular depictions of the pre-fall paradise as being free from work is proven to be blatantly false according to Scripture and a denial of man's created purpose. Mankind was created to work, and work was to be a form of worship unto God. In its pre-fall context, work was fulfilling.

In regard to understanding the nature of work as worship, work was and is very much religious, and this is because all of what man does has a *directional* religious orientation, it is either done vertically in worship of God (true worship), or horizontally in worship of creation (idolatry). The former is true worship, while the latter is *apostasy*. What is apostasy? Apostasy, from the Greek word *apostasia* (ἀποστασία), can be defined as standing *away* from the truth, as opposed to standing *in* the truth. It is a falling away from the truth, a *spiritual death* that results from seeking one's being and origin within the temporal created order instead of the Creator.

It is principally why there are countless religious worldviews in our day, but more on that matter later. Given this religious dynamic of work, which naturally follows from the religious nature of man, it was the American Christian philosopher H. Evan Runner who said "Life is Religion", or to put it another way, "Life is *Worship*." There can be nothing truly *irreligious* in the life of man.

If, therefore, work is religious, then it makes logical sense for work to become *apostatic* as a result of man's fall into sin, and for work to become apostatic, there can only follow the consequences of man's apostasy. In Genesis 3:17-19, God made clear to Adam that the work that he had once enjoyed and found much ease and fulfillment in performing would now come under the curse of sin. This was God's judgment:

> …"Because you have listened to the voice of your wife
>> and have eaten of the tree
> of which I commanded you,
>> 'You shall not eat of it,'
> cursed is the ground because of you;

> in pain you shall eat of it all the days of your
> life;
> thorns and thistles it shall bring forth for you;
> and you shall eat the plants of the field.
> By the sweat of your face
> you shall eat bread,
> till you return to the ground,
> for out of it you were taken;
> for you are dust,
> and to dust you shall return."

Work, in other words, would become *toil*. Toil, as defined by the Merriam Webster Dictionary, is "long strenuous fatiguing labour." How might we understand toil? Let's put this into perspective: *Growing food* would become difficult. *Finding food* would become difficult. *Labour* would become difficult. *Marriage* would become difficult. *Procreating* would become difficult. *Staying healthy* would become difficult. You name it, *Life* would become difficult. And *death*, which entered the world right behind sin, would prove to be unbearably difficult. We can attest to this reality because we are presently living under the curse of sin, and so none of this proves to be a surprise to us, it all corresponds with what we know and experience. And it is in this fallen reality that we know, deep down in our hearts, that things are not as they ought to be. Our work, our *lives*, are not as fulfilling as they ought to be, not as meaningful as they ought to be. There is a dullness that has gripped us, and we cannot seem to awake from it. A slumber which has overtaken us. This dullness, this slumber, is the feeling of meaninglessness, like we have lost our true direction, our true purpose, our true selves. We labour day in and day out, do our part until we bite the dust, and then someone else will come and go at it again. Those who have amassed wealth will see it outlive them, and those who have not laboured will inherit wealth that was not the result of their own doing. Great accomplishments will give way to greater accomplishments, and our efforts to be remembered will be in vain as we are forgotten in time. Empires of dirt, erected over the course of our lives, will be just that, mounds of dirt, and it will all come crumbling down to nothing. The musician Johnny Cash had something to say about that in his song "Hurt":

> …Beneath the stains of time
> The feelings disappear

You are someone else
I'm still right here

What have I become?
My sweetest friend
Everyone I know goes away
In the end

And you could have it all
My empire of dirt…

Work, as you can begin to see, is more than just a 9-5 job on weekdays. It is the story of our lives, it's our living, breathing, and thinking, and it has *all* become subjected to futility. To quote the Preacher in the wisdom book of Ecclesiastes:

Vanity of vanities, says the Preacher,
    vanity of vanities! All is vanity.
What does man gain by all the toil
    at which he toils under the sun?
A generation goes, and a generation comes,
    but the earth remains forever.
The sun rises, and the sun goes down,
    and hastens to the place where it rises.
The wind blows to the south
    and goes around to the north;
around and around goes the wind,

and on its circuits the wind returns.
All streams run to the sea,
    but the sea is not full;
to the place where the streams flow,
    there they flow again.
All things are full of weariness;
    a man cannot utter it;
the eye is not satisfied with seeing,
    nor the ear filled with hearing.
What has been is what will be,
    and what has been done is what will be done,
    and there is nothing new under the sun.
Is there a thing of which it is said,
    "See, this is new"?
It has been already
    in the ages before us.
There is no remembrance of former things,
    nor will there be any remembrance
of later things yet to be
    among those who come after (Ecc. 1:2-11).

What a sorrowful state of things. How sin has so radically altered the state of things. And without a doubt, this matter of vanity (Eccl. 1:2) is not excluded from the effects of sin upon the threefold call of man.

The Effects of Sin upon the Threefold Call of Man

As a result of mankind's fall, the creational (cultural) mandate was compromised. Having violated the peace he had (i) with God, (ii) with his fellow man, and (iii) with creation, man's attempts to cultivate a godly civilization in his own strength would prove to be a vain endeavour. His every attempt would be hampered by the power and influence of sin, and thus it is no wonder that though this was attempted through the line of Seth (Gen. 4:6), it became undone when it mixed with the line of Cain (Gen. 6:1-5). More on these "two seeds" in the next chapter. With the inception of sin, no longer would man prove uniform (in agreement) with the a-normative aspects (the violable laws, in contrast to those *normative* laws that cannot be violated), no more would he find himself in perfect compliance with those creational law-spheres. Does this mean that man's threefold call as prophet, priest, and king was abolished? To abolish such a call would be to abolish man altogether, the call and the created being of man are inseparable. Instead, what occurred was that man ceased from being the prophet, priest, and

45

king *of God*, and became *his own* prophet, priest, and king. To put it another way, man became *the measure of all things*. At least, that is what the natural man (or the apostate, Cf. 1 Cor. 2:14) portrays himself to be.

In regard to man as his own prophet, instead of interpreting creation according to the revelation of God, or with God as the ultimate reference point, man has attempted to redefine reality by means of his own reinterpretation. Today's redefinition of marriage, sexuality, gender, life, the human person, justice, etc., are all the byproducts of man operating as his own prophet. And the longer this progresses (or *regresses* from the original state of things) the closer society inches towards its inevitable cultural implosion. Why is that? Because the more we move away from absolutes and towards relativism, and the more we drift from God's truth and towards man's fallen fantasies, the more we sink into nihilistic (meaningless) futility. And within such nihilism, everything loses its meaning. While certainly alarming, this is *not* a novel development (Eccl. 1:9), man has operated as his own prophet since the fall. This explains the numerous religious worldviews that have come and gone throughout human history and the plethora of religious worldviews that exist today. Contrary to the theories of apostate intellectuals, religion did not evolve from some basic primitive form (i.e., mana, animism, etc.), it began as worship of the one true God, referred to as *original monotheism*. And from that origin point there was a falling away (apostasy) which resulted in varying deviations.[8] Deviations which are nothing more than counterfeits of the truth. As the apostle Paul writes in his letter to the church in Rome, mankind in his fallen disposition exchanged the worship of God for creation:

> For although they knew God, they did not honor him as God or give thanks to him, but they became futile in their thinking, and their foolish hearts were darkened. Claiming to be wise, they became

8. Studies by Wilhelm Schmidt and Winfried Corduan respectively demonstrate how history and its artifacts align with the biblical narrative. See Schmidt, *The Origin and Growth of Religions: Facts and Theories*, trans. H.J. Rose (Wythe-North Publishing, 2014); Corduan, *In the Beginning God: A Fresh Look at the Case for Original Monotheism* (Nashville, TN.: B&H Academic, 2013).

> fools, and exchanged the glory of the immortal God for images resembling mortal man and birds and animals and creeping things (Rom. 1:21-23).

Man operating as his own prophet has brought about more harm than good. And no matter how hard he may try, this will never change.

In regard to man as his own priest, instead of consecrating all of creation — and all that man develops from it — unto God, he dedicates it all unto himself. It is no secret that we live in a self-centered world. If there was an *ism* that we could use to describe the religio-cultural reality of the world, it would be *selfism*. Man is the center of all things; he is the *measure* of all things. Love of self has triumphed over love of God and neighbour. This is the result of man's sin, it is the very nature of sin. For man to be the center of all things means that he has become his own god, the original, sinful intention of our first parents when they ate from the forbidden tree. And this is true for all who have fallen away, irregardless of what religious worldview they may profess. Whether it be the atheist who believes in a godless universe, the Muslim who believes in Allah, the Hindu who believes in Krishna

48

and the rest of the Hindu pantheon, irregardless of the name or the gods (or lack thereof), man is the new god because he has replaced the true God with himself as the ultimate judge and determiner of reality. To put it more simply, he has made himself the ultimate authority, subject to no one. This has been expressed in various forms, whether individually, or collectively such as in the form of the state. Not that there is anything wrong with the institution of the state itself, only that when the state is not made subject to God, it becomes His replacement, the idol of collectivized man. Of course, this selfism produces perpetual, never-ending conflict between man, and even man's attempt to resolve this by means of altruism proves to be in vain since it is ultimately rooted in selfism (e.g., to do good for another in order for oneself to feel good). We are inevitably led to ask, Who is more important? Who is to be prioritized over whom? Whose life holds more value? Whose rights are to be respected above the others? Selfism, the worship of the self, has not brought about unity, it has brought about division, fragmentation, and continual animosity.

In regard to man as his own king, instead of

governing creation subject to the rule and law of God, man has rejected the kingship of God in favour of his own kingship. In his radical autonomy, he has become his own law and has freed himself from all moral restraints. It is not God who establishes what is good and evil, it is man who arbitrarily decides this, and as history testifies, the distinction between what is good and evil has changed innumerable times without any guiding principle. A postgraduate student once told me, for example, that the moral law of society is determined by who wins the world's wars. If Nazi Germany had won World War II, then according to his logic, our morality would have been fashioned according to Nazi ideology. When I pressed him as to whether he thought this would be wrong, he said the only reason he could say that such morality would be wrong is because Nazi Germany had lost the war. And for that reason he condemns it. But had they won, he would have no reason to condemn such morality. This "morality", mind you, justified the Holocaust (1941-1945), the genocide of European Jews, amongst other atrocities. The thought put forward by this student should be repulsive, and yet, it is the inevitable result of man being his own king. The man, or the collectivized man (the state), with the most power determines the moral social order. Woe to the man who is weaker than the rest.

Over the course of human history, what we have seen, and what we will continue to see so long as man remains in his apostasy, is his total depravation, disorganization, and decomposition. And that brings us to the overall state of creation.

The State of Creation

Prior to the fall of man, everything was declared to be "good" by God. What happened that altered the state of things? Mankind sinned against God. And because creation was made subject to man, when the curse of sin was laid upon man, it was also laid upon creation (Rom. 8:20). It is for this reason that we see in our world: sickness, suffering, and death. These were not originally present in creation, they were consequences of the fall. Man, for example, was to live forever. Ecclesiastes 3:11 says "[God] has put eternity into man's heart…" This is why we feel so strongly about death, it is foreign to creation. Death is like an invading enemy with a 10 for 10

51

kill rate. Nothing in our fallen world is untouched by the tyranny of death. Every living creature is subject to it. And this will remain so for as long as there is sin in the world.

Before this great enemy of death there stands a resistance and a helplessness. First, the resistance lies in our unwillingness to accept our own mortality, although for the natural man it is often his unwillingness to accept his sentencing. Death, after all, is a part of God's judgment, and it is a reminder of the final judgment that awaits (Matt. 25:31-46; Acts 2:27; 2 Peter 3:3-7). What this resistance looks like is varied. In Mexico, for example, there is a cultural striving to be remembered beyond this earthly life, because it is said that as long as you live on in people's memories, you *never really die*. That might remind you of the Disney movie *Coco*, which was inspired by Mexican culture and its pagan beliefs. And those who are left behind in the land of the living make it a point to remember the dead, erecting for them altars where they can offer up food and drink. The Netflix biopic of Vicente Fernández, *El Rey*, illustrates this religio-cultural practice. Meanwhile, in the West, efforts are well underway to help man discover the means of transcending his own mortality. One of the ways in which this has taken form has been with the *transhumanist* movement, defined as "the belief or theory that the human race can evolve beyond its current physical and mental limitations, especially by means of science and technology."[9] What man desires deep down is to return to the original state of things, *but on his own terms.*

Immortality? That quest since the fall is nothing but vanity. And while the rebellious intent of sin is always present, and we should not lose sight of that fact, it cannot be denied that there is also a deep sadness, a hopelessness, a helplessness, which is the second point, because no matter what man may attempt, he cannot manufacture such a return, he cannot solve the problem of his own mortality. Science fiction movies like *Transcendence* starring Johnny Depp, or *Lucy* starring Scarlett Johanson, remain just what they are, *fiction* and *wishful thinking* at best. Yet they identify and communicate a sadness in the human heart. What is the *cause* of

---

9. See David Herbert, *Becoming God: Transhumanism and the Quest for Cybernetic Immortality* (Peterborough, ON.: Joshua Press, 2014).

this sadness? The answer is found in that yearning that lies in our heart of hearts (yes, even after the poisoning of sin) for renewal. For a restoration of the state of things. That, at least, was not robbed of us by our sin. We look upon the world, we look upon humanity, we look upon the state of things, and we see its brokenness, its twistedness, its fall-enness. Creation appears as in need of redemption. WE appear as in need of redemption. But that redemption cannot be wrought by the hands of men. We desperately need some good news.

Chapter Four

REDEMPTION

*"For if while we were enemies we were
reconciled to God by the death of his Son,
much more, now that we are reconciled,
shall we be saved by his life."*
– Romans 5:10

WHAT WAS DONE TO REMEDY the alteration? Firstly, given that it was man who brought about the fall of God's "good" creation, God was under no obligation to remedy what man had altered. If God so decided, He could have left us to our own devices, which would have resulted in us walking to our own destruction and eventual extinction. Or, God could have wiped us out in the twinkling of an eye; after all, He had every right to do so. And yet, neither of those two scenarios played out over the course of history. The Bible, instead, recounts a very *different* story, one which is still unfolding today.

When man was confronted by God for his first and most foundational sin, what theologians have called "original sin" (Gen. 3; Ps. 51:5; Rom. 5:12-21), God promised man that He would provide, by means of the woman's offspring, a Redeemer who would crush the head of the serpent, the latter of which our first parents understood to be Satan, as well as everything he represented and all that he had caused. As biblical scholar Barry Cooper defines him:

> [Satan] is a being created by God, who… rebelled against the Creator. (Jesus says, "I saw Satan fall like lightning from heaven.") He is engaged in constant warfare against God and all those God has created. According to the Bible, one of his aims is to turn men and women against their loving Creator, thus luring them to destruction. He is said in Scripture to speak, to lie, to work, to struggle against God's angels, to desire, to prowl, to have designs and plans to outwit believers, to blind the minds of unbeliev-

ers, to murder, to get angry, and to deceive.[1]

Adam and Eve, our first parents, thought that this promise from God spoke of an immediate future, in other words, that one of their own sons would have fulfilled this redeeming role. This anticipation is expressed soon after Abel's death at the hands of his brother Cain (Gen. 4:1-15). Since Abel was dead, and Cain had been cursed to wander the earth, Adam and Eve gave the next son they bore the name "Seth" (Gen. 4:25), which meant "appointed." Was Seth the appointed one? Was he the promised fulfillment of the first redemptive prophecy (Gen. 3:15)? Adam and Eve must have thought so, but he was no different than any of his other brothers and sisters. He too was affected by the fall.

However, there did proceed from these two sons of Adam the contrasting lines (or seeds) I had mentioned in the previous chapter, the line of Cain (the seed of the serpent) and the line of Seth (the seed of God).[2] We are not given specifics, but from

---

1. Barry Cooper, "Satan", *Ligonier.* Accessed Jan. 26, 2023, https://www.ligonier.org/podcasts/simply-put/satan/.

2. It was the church father St. Augustine (AD 354-

what we can derive from Scripture, Cain and his
descendants formed a godless civilization. Remember, man's call and creational purpose was to cultivate creation into a godly civilization. That call
was not annulled by sin, since it is rooted in the
creational purpose of man, but it has been *corrupted*
by sin. Given that fact, with Cain there then arose
a godless civilization, and we see evidence of this in
Genesis 4:16-24. However, with Seth there arose an
attempt at a godly civilization (Gen. 4:26). Those
of the line (or seed) of Cain were called "sons/
daughters of man" (Gen. 6:1), while those of the
line (or seed) of Seth were called "sons/daughters of
God" (Gen. 6:2). Eventually, the two lines mixed
into one, as we read in Genesis 6:2, "the sons of
God saw that the daughters of man were attractive.

430) who wrote that "Adam was the father of both
lines — the father, that is to say, both of the line
which belonged to the earthly, and of that which
belonged to the heavenly city — when Abel was
slain... there were henceforth two lines proceeding
from two fathers, Cain and Seth, and in those sons
of theirs, whom it behooved to register, the tokens
of these two cities began to appear more distinctly", in *The City of God*, Book XV, Chapter XVII.

And they took as their wives any they chose." One might think that all had been lost (Gen. 6:3), that the line or seed from which the Redeemer would come had become compromised, but the plan of redemption was never man's to begin with, nor was it up to man to perform the work that was exclusively God's. What God did was preserve the distinction between the godly and the wicked, despite the appeared mixing of the two lines (Gen. 6:2, 8). He preserved the seed of the faithful, as we see with the later setting apart of Noah and his family (Gen. 6:8-10).

In this particular instance of history, that being the Noahic account, God hinted not only at what is *yet to come* (the catastrophic flood served as a sign of coming judgment), but what He was *going to do* (the ark that housed Noah and his family, as well as two of every *kind* of the beasts of the earth and creatures of the air, served as a sign of God's salvation). From the line of Noah's son, Shem (Gen. 11:10-32), after the events of Babel, God also set apart a man named Abram, giving him the name "Abraham", which meant "the father of many nations", through whom God would raise up a people for Himself. These people, who have as their patriarchs Abraham, Isaac, and Jacob, and who were descendants of Noah, and sons of Adam, were called "Hebrews" during their captivity in Egypt, but as God's people they were called "Israel" (Exod. 1:1).[3] Not only had God promised that Abraham's descendants would be as numerous as the stars (Gen. 15:5), He had also promised His descendants the land of Canaan: "And I will give to you and to your offspring after you the land of your sojournings, all the land of Canaan, for an everlasting possession, and *I will be their God*" (Gen. 17:8, italicism mine.)

When we look at the Exodus story that follows, we see again the manifestation of God's grace in delivering a people that He had set apart for Himself, similar to how God demonstrated His grace in the account of the Patriarchs (Gen. 12:10-20; 26:6-35; 33), and prior to that, stretching back to the Garden of Eden. And just as we can see those earlier manifestations of His grace, we also see hints

---

3. Jacob had been given the name "Israel" by God (Gen. 35:10), towards the end of Genesis and in the opening of Exodus, the Hebrews are referred to as sons of Israel.

or glimpses of God's intentions in the unfolding of history. The slavery of the Hebrews in Egypt, for example, served as a reflection of our enslavement to sin; the exodus of the Hebrews from Egypt served as a reflection of God's future (and present) deliverance of His people; the sojourn of the people in the wilderness served as a reflection of our earthly pilgrimage of faith; and the receiving of the Promised Land was a reflection of the culmination of God's promise to bring the people to total restoration and renewal. These we understand to be signs of the redemptive work of God for those who have repented and exercised their gift of faith, and who are now called His people (the greater *spiritual* Israel), irrespective of ethnicity (See Gen. 12:2-3; Matt. 8:11; Rom. 11:11-24; Matt. 28:18-20). This redemptive unfolding is what we see in the Torah, or in the Pentateuch (the first five books of the Law in the Old Testament). Throughout the rest of the Old Testament we witness several other signs of God's redemptive plan unfolding, and at risk of oversimplifying the narrative, but being mindful that this chapter is not meant to be a survey of the Old Testament, what can be said is this: that man

61

demonstrated himself to be incapable of bringing about his own redemption, as is witnessed in Israel's numerous failings. But nonetheless, through the nation of Israel, from the line of King David whom God had made a covenant with, God would provide the promised Redeemer, the promised seed (2 Sam. 7:12-13; 1 Chron. 17:11-14; 2 Chron. 6:16). And it was necessary, given man's own inability, that this Redeemer be more than just a man, but *God Himself.* This is why the fourth century church father, St. Athanasius, conveyed that:

> [O]nly the assumption of humanity by one who is himself fully divine could effect a change in this creaturely state; by becoming human and living a human life, the divine Word, who is in himself the true image of God, restored the image of God that is marred in us.[4]

This event of the coming of the Redeemer brings us into the New Testament. It must be

---

4. Ivor J. Davidson. *A Public Faith: From Constantine to the Medieval World AD 312-600*, ed. John D. Woodbridge, David F. Wright, and Tim Dowley, Volume Two. (Grand Rapids: Baker Books, 2005), 64.

noted, however, prior to proceeding further, that since I have used the word "grace" to describe this unfolding narrative, that it would be best to explain what that term means. "Grace" (Gr. χάρις), as we understand it biblically, is God's unmerited favour toward man. And this grace has been displayed since the moment that Adam and Eve first received the redemptive promise, to the moment they were given garments made of skins (implying a sacrifice of atonement, see Gen. 3:21), to the moment that Noah and his family were saved from the catastrophic flood, to the moment that Abraham and the subsequent nation of Israel were set apart as God's people, and to the moment that God brought into the world the promised Redeemer. And God's grace is evident *still* when we consider that the Redeemer has not yet completed His work (2 Pet. 3:9). He is still at work today redeeming creation. In every instance, man has been the beneficiary, and in every instance, man has been, and is *undeserving*. That is what makes it "grace." This is why the former slave merchant turned abolitionist and Anglican cleric, John Newton (1725-1807), wrote in his famous hymn, *Amazing Grace*:

Amazing grace (how sweet the sound)
that saved a wretch like me!
I once was lost, but now am found,
was blind, but now I see

'Twas grace that taught my heart to fear
And grace my fears relieved
How precious did that grace appear
The hour I first believed

Through many dangers, toils, and snares
I have already come
This grace that brought me safe thus far
And grace will lead me home....

Everything in the Law and the Prophets, everything in the Old Testament, pointed towards the
coming of the Redeemer, the fulfillment of God's
promise in Genesis 3:15. It was at that moment,
and it remains so today, the "gospel", the "good
news" as announced by the angel of the Lord on
that blessed night when the Redeemer was born.

> ..."Fear not, for behold, I bring you good news of
> great joy that will be for all the people. For unto you
> is born this day in the city of David a Savior, who is
> Christ the Lord. And this will be a sign for you: you

will find a baby wrapped in swaddling cloths and lying in a manger" (Lk. 2:10-12).

The Redeemer

Who is the Redeemer? Who is the promised seed? Jesus the Christ, the incarnate Son of God.[5] In John 3:16 we are told that

> For God so loved the world, that he gave his only Son, that whoever believes in him should not perish but have eternal life.

In the whole of Scripture we see the Triune God, the Father, Son, and Holy Spirit: three Persons, one Being. It is the Son who is sent by the Father to take on bodily form in order to fulfill the redemptive role that only *He* can fulfill. And the Spirit applies the work of the Son to those whom God sets apart (as evidenced by their faith, see Matt. 7:15-20; Jn. 14:16-17; Eph. 2:5). The arrival of the Son is of such significance, and the significance of such magnitude, that He divides history into two parts, not

---

5. See Robert M. Bowman and J. Ed Komoszewski, *Putting Jesus in His Place: The Case for the Deity of Christ* (Grand Rapids, MI.: Kregel Publications).

only between Old and New Testaments, but between the eras of BC (Before Christ) and AD (*Anno Domini,* Latin for "the Year of the Lord"). We can certainly argue about what year *exactly* Christ was born, but regardless as to where we might land, the coming of the Christ began the *Anno Domini.*

What exactly did Jesus accomplish? Firstly, He succeeds where our first parents had failed, in terms of our required obedience to God. And for this reason, and given the unique role that He occupies as the God-man (fully God, fully man) and Redeemer, He is called the "last (or second) Adam" (1 Cor. 15:45). To put it simply, the Redeemer must be one who can fulfill the Law of God in its fullness, something Israel could never do, in order to offer Himself up as an atoning sacrifice for the sins of mankind. That is what the Old Testament ceremonial laws and sacrifices pointed towards: the lamb without blemish who takes away the sins of the world (Jn. 1:29). And how would He do this exactly? This is the second point: By paying the sin debt we all owed: death. The Bible teaches that the wages of sin is death (Rom. 6:23). Moses, in Exodus 32:30-34, had once offered up himself in exchange for the salvation of God's people in the wilderness. The offer was never accepted, of course, because he could not fulfill the requirements (1 Pet. 2:22-24). But it was a sign that one greater than Moses would come, and His offer would not be rejected. Jesus is that greater one, the one who fulfilled all the requirements. He was perfectly righteous, and by nature divine, and thus not only could He pay for the sins of all those who have repented and believed, He could affect a change in them, an undoing of the "radical reversal" caused by sin.

It is true that historically, the Jews of Jesus' time had expected a military figure of a Messiah in order to liberate them from their subjugation to Rome. They had their own nationalistic ambitions, and Josephus' *The Fall of Jerusalem* recounts what those ambitions cost them. But what Jesus came to do was far greater than what the Jews of the time had thought possible: He came to liberate man from his sin (Lk. 4:18-21), and to deliver creation from its subjugation to sin's curse (Jn. 8:34-36). And to accomplish that end, death was necessary. In other words, the promised seed was born in order that He might die. Consider the irony: He who is life was born to die, so that by His death He could bring new life. To paraphrase the thought of C.S. Lewis, the gospel is not a story that you would ever expect mankind to invent.

But I must add an important fact at this point, because otherwise people would claim that we worship a "dead God." That statement cannot be further from the truth, we worship a living God. It is true that historically, Jesus Christ was crucified and died an excruciating death at the hands of the Romans, but it is equally true that on the third day after His death, Jesus was raised from the dead. Who raised Jesus from the dead? John 2:19 tells us that the *Son* raised up His own life. Galatians 1:1 states that the *Father* raised Him from the dead. 1 Peter 3:18 states that the *Holy Spirit* raised Him from the dead. There is no contradiction. These three persons are the one and the same God, so it is rightly said that *God* raised Him from the dead. And if it were not for the resurrection, then all that Jesus accomplished would have been in vain. In fact, we would be the people to be the most pitied. Our faith rests and falls on the resurrection of the Christ (1 Cor. 15:12-20). If Christ was not raised, then what is the point? But Christ did in fact rise from the grave. And because He arose, we have *new life*.

In the previous chapter, we learned that the fall of man resulted in our spiritual death. Only God can give life to the dead. The prophet Ezekiel saw a vision of a valley of dry bones being restored to a living people (Ezek. 37), such is the life that God gives to our beings, and which He promises more fully at the end of created time. Read what Ezekiel says:

> The hand of the Lord was upon me, and he brought me out in the Spirit of the Lord and set me down in the middle of the valley; it was full of bones. And he led me around among them, and behold, there were very many on the surface of the valley, and behold, they were very dry. And he said to me, "Son of man, can these bones live?" And I answered, "O Lord God, you know." Then he said to me, "Prophesy over these bones, and say to them, O dry bones, hear the word of the Lord. Thus says the Lord God to these bones: Behold, I will cause breath to enter you, and you shall live. And I will lay sinews upon you, and will cause flesh to come upon you, and cover you with skin, and put breath in you, and

you shall live, and you shall know that I am the Lord." So I prophesied as I was commanded. And as I prophesied, there was a sound, and behold, a rattling, and the bones came together, bone to its bone. And I looked, and behold, there were sinews on them, and flesh had come upon them, and skin had covered them. But there was no breath in them. Then he said to me, "Prophesy to the breath; prophesy, son of man, and say to the breath, Thus says the Lord God: Come from the four winds, O breath, and breathe on these slain, that they may live." So I prophesied as he commanded me, and the breath came into them, and they lived and stood on their feet, an exceedingly great army. Then he said to me, "Son of man, these bones are the whole house of Israel. Behold, they say, 'Our bones are dried up, and our hope is lost; we are indeed cut off.' Therefore prophesy, and say to them, Thus says the Lord God: Behold, I will open your graves and raise you from your graves, O my people. And I will bring you into the land of Israel. And you shall know that I am the Lord, when I open your graves, and raise you from your graves, O my people. And I will put my Spirit within you, and you shall live, and I will place you in your own land. Then you shall know that I am the Lord; I have spoken, and I will do it, declares the Lord" (Ezek. 37:1-14).

This prophetic vision would be realized in the Christ. How? When Jesus Christ was crucified on the cross, it was to bear our iniquities, our sin. And while He hung there on that tree (Gal. 3:13), the wrath of God was poured out on Him in full. The wrath that is reserved for the wicked, the wrath of a just and holy God that was meant for you and me, was taken on in its fullness by Jesus Christ. He *literally* became our scapegoat. In fact, that is where we get the concept of "scapegoat" from. A righteous and innocent person suffered in the place of the sinful party. By doing so, Jesus satisfied the wrath of God, what theologians refer to as the *propitiation* of our sins, and He cancelled out the sin of His people, what they call the work of *expiation*. That cancellation is eternal in its consequence, even though sin is still present in the *temporal* sense. In other words, those who repent and believe have been delivered from the penalty and power of sin, *though not yet from the presence of it.* And by taking away our sins, the Spirit of God applies to us the righteousness of the Christ, also referred to as *imputed righteousness.* With this exchange, that being our sin for His righteousness, we are justified before God in the eyes of the Law. Furthermore, we are given spiritual life. And being spiritually alive, we are being continually *sanctified* by the Spirit of God.

What does sanctification mean? Sanctification is the ongoing process whereby those who repent and believe are delivered from the power of sin and are enabled by their new nature to resist and turn away from it. To be sanctified by the Spirit of God presupposes a new nature. Our nature was originally good before the fall because we were created in the image of God, but the fall resulted in a radical reversal of our nature, from a disposition of righteousness to unrighteousness. But, when the Spirit of God gives us life, enabling us to repent and believe in the Son, we are then given a new nature. The old is crucified to the cross with Christ, and the new is raised with Christ as He rose from the dead (Rom. 6:4; Col. 2:12). This new nature birthed by the Spirit is the new life given to us by God, and it is in the image of the Son.

These wonderful, biblical truths already speak

volumes about the depths and riches of the grace of God, but there is yet more to be said. When the Spirit of God gives us new life in the Son, we are also made *children of God*. That is right, we are not left as orphans, and no longer are we children of the devil (1 Jn. 3:10). As the apostle Paul writes:

> But when the fullness of time had come, God sent forth his Son, born of woman, born under the law, to redeem those who were under the law, so that we might receive adoption as sons (Gal. 4:4-5).

Again, we see the distinction, the contrast, between the two seeds running throughout the course of history: that of the serpent (Satan), and that of God. Or to use St. Augustine's terminology from his *magnum opus, The City of God*: "the city of man" and "the city of God." The two are not destined to be in conflict with each other *forever*. This is not similar to the endless cycle portrayed by the Greek tale of Sisyphus. Over time, the city of God will grow greater and will triumph on the day of Christ's return, while the city of man will diminish and will eventually be done away with. More on that toward the end.

What then did Jesus accomplish? If in the beginning there was peace between man and God, man and his fellow man, and man and creation, and sin brought about violence to that threefold relationship and altered the state of things, what Jesus came to do was to restore what had been lost: *Shalom* (peace).

The Restoration of the Threefold Relationship

Ever since the fall, man has been an enemy of God (Rom. 5:10; 8:7-21). His heart, though originally created upright and in harmony with his Creator, had been twisted by sin and marked by a deranged hostility against God and His law (Rom. 8:7). As we have seen, instead of willfully bowing to God's sovereignty, he has rejected His rule in favour of setting up his own throne and kingdom. What he seeks is what our first parents had sought in the beginning, his own complete independence from the Creator, *radical autonomy*. He is, in fact, in love with it. And because of this love of sin, by his own strength, man cannot break free from the shackles of his own addiction. And because he cannot remove these shackles, he therefore cannot shake off his own hostility. He knows deep down that he is wrong, that the God who created the heavens and earth is perfect and just, but he is powerless to do anything about it, he is at the mercy of his own sin nature. There is, therefore, violence in his heart against God, it is devoid of all peace. But with the coming of the Christ, an otherwise hopeless situation becomes hopeful, because Christ came to make peace between man and God. Justice still had to be done, that is why Jesus went to the cross on our behalf, but by coming in the form of man and doing what He did, He provided the means for peace to be restored, those means being *His death on the cross*. But this peace is not yet applied and put into effect until the Spirit of God first touches the heart of man. When the Spirit does this, He brings life to where there was death, He gives sight to where there was blindness, and He gives faith to where there was faithlessness. By doing these things, the Spirit of God enables man to respond to the call of the Redeemer, to repent and turn away from all sin and to surrender and follow Him in faith. When this change occurs, when the sinner is touched by the Spirit of God and responds to that now irresistible call of God, the redemptive work of Jesus Christ is applied and put into full effect. Where there was once violence and hostility, there is now peace. Peace between man and God, for on the one side, man has humbled himself before God's sovereignty, and on the other side, God's justice has been satisfied. And not willing for us to be orphans, as I had mentioned, He adopts us as His children, bringing us back into the fellowship that our first parents had lost. No longer does the curtain of separation mark the separation between man and God (Matt. 27:51). The separation has been bridged, and His name is Jesus Christ. Peace, *Shalom*, has been restored. If what Adam and Eve experienced before the fall was "Paradise", in regard to their relationship with God, then what Jesus accomplished on Golgotha, the mount where Jesus was crucified, was the re-establishment of "Paradise" (Lk. 23:43). What was it that Jesus said to the converted criminal who was crucified alongside him? "Truly, I say to you, today you will be with me in paradise." That "Paradise", that restored communion, is a now and not yet reality. It is *now* in the sense that we now

76

have access to the throne of God, by the grace of God, as a son has access to his father.[6] And it is *not yet* because we still await the day when we can walk with God totally unencumbered, and when we can experience Him in all His fullness on the new earth, where heaven and earth have become one (Rev. 21-22).

As for the relationship between man and fellow man, that too experiences a restoration of *Shalom* as a result of what Jesus accomplished on the cross. When peace is restored between man and God, the love that is birthed on the side of man toward God (because God never stopped loving His creation) is also extended to fellow man. Man cannot love his fellow man if he does not first love God. In fact, the state of his relationship to fellow man is always determined by the state of his relationship to God. For example: In his sin, the natural man hates God, and as result, it can be said that in his sin, man hates

6. See John Hultink, *Golgotha: The Turning Point in History* (Jordan Station, ON.: Paideia Press, 2020).; Timothy Mackie and Jonathan Collins, *When Heaven Meets Earth* (Portland, OR.: The Bible Project).

fellow man. The good he happens to do for another is either done for some self-seeking purpose, or it is done in spite of himself, which is very much likely considering that the image of God has not been totally expunged from our beings but has simply been marred. But in Christ, who restores in us the image of God, man cannot help but love fellow man. What is love? How is this love expressed? The apostle Paul explains what this love looks like in 1 Corinthians 13:4-7:

> Love is patient and kind; love does not envy or boast; it is not arrogant or rude. It does not insist on its own way; it is not irritable or resentful; it does not rejoice at wrongdoing, but rejoices with the truth. Love bears all things, believes all things, hopes all things, endures all things.

This love is certainly expressed within the context of marriage and the family, hence why it is cited at weddings. But it is also expressed within the context of God's community (the church), and within the context of our common living with man. As a matter of fact, the formation of the new *spiritual* Israel, that being the church, consisting of people of all nations and tongues (Matt. 8:11; Rom. 11:11-31), is the result of the restoration of peace between fellow man. It is the new society that God has birthed by the power of the resurrection of the Christ, a society that will one day encompass the whole earth in its entirety, the triumph of the "City of God." Until then, that new society, being the church, is to love the world (that is, the people, not the fallen world system) by proclaiming the gospel and administering its graces, with the anticipation that God will apply the redemptive work of Christ to others and add "to [our] number day by day those... being saved" (Acts 2:47). In regard to the administration of gospel graces, or put differently, the love expressed to fellow man and what that looks like, St. Augustine, in a phrase often attributed to him, says the following:

> What does love look like? It has the hands to help others. It has the feet to hasten to the poor and needy. It has eyes to see misery and want. It has the ears to hear the sighs and sorrows of men. That is what love looks like.

Does it sound like I am saying that there is no

love outside of God? Yes, that is what I am saying. There is no love outside of the gospel, there cannot be, sin assures us of that. Over and against what the world might say, love is not a fleeting feeling. Love is more so a verb than it is a noun, because it has more to do with acting than feeling. And that love is maximally expressed in the sacrifice of Jesus Christ. In the Garden of Gethsemane, when He prayed to the Father for strength in preparation for the great sacrifice, Jesus went ahead with His redemptive plan, not because He *felt* like dying for our sins, but because He *chose* to. In John 15:13, Jesus Himself said, "Greater love has no one than this, that someone lay down his life for his friends." It is because of the love of God that we can love our fellow man, for otherwise, how can we love if we know not love?

As it concerns man's relationship to creation, this too experiences a restoration of *Shalom*. While what Jesus accomplished on the cross was primarily for our salvation and redemption, the significance of His sacrifice goes beyond our "spiritual" condition and extends to everything we do in the here and now. By forgiving repentant man his trespasses, by giving him new life and freedom from sin, what Jesus did in essence was enable man to take up his creational purpose again, but this time, with the *potential* to now fulfill it as it was meant to be. Remember, man was originally tasked with tending the Garden, cultivating it into a godly civilization. That task, that call, is renewed in Christ. We might put it this way: If in Adam, who was given dominion, all fell into sin, and therefore all failed to exercise dominion in the way that it ought to have been, then in Christ, the new Dominion man, all are made alive, and all are enabled to exercise dominion as they were originally meant to (Gen. 1:28).

But, of course, when we think of *Shalom* being restored to our relationship with creation, we think more about the state of creation than what we are called to do with it. We all still experience sickness and suffering, we all still age and will die, the futility highlighted by the Preacher in Ecclesiastes is still evident to us all. But here is the good news: it is all temporary. When Jesus came to the world, He set things in motion, and when He returns, He will finish what He started. We are, in the meantime, in that interim period between the two advents (comings of the Christ). How long will it be? We do not know. Scripture is silent on that matter. But what we do know is that the clock is winding down, the time is coming when all things will be made new by the Son (1 Cor. 15:20-58; Rev. 12:12). How? When? Why don't we see that as clearly as we would like to? Those are questions that I will try to address further below.

How This Relates to the Creational Mandate

How does what Jesus accomplished through His life, death, and resurrection relate to the creational mandate? In the first chapter I had mentioned how Adam was to be the prophet, priest and king of God. And in the second chapter, I explained how Adam failed to fulfill his mandate because of his sin. The mandate persisted, but no man could fulfill it, until Jesus that is. As the God-man, Jesus came to fulfill what man could not fulfill, not just so He could secure for us our salvation (this is not just some hell-insurance), but so He could restore to us our true purpose and call. How was this done? Firstly, Jesus came as God's prophet, to interpret creation after God. Secondly, He came as God's priest, to consecrate creation unto God. And thirdly, He came as God's King, to govern creation subject to the law and rule of God. The three gifts He received from the wise men in His infancy, of myrrh, frankincense, and gold, were symbolic of this threefold office of prophet, priest, and king (Matt. 2:11). As I had stated earlier, Jesus came as the new "Dominion" man, as the second Adam, and not only did He provide the means for us to receive new life, He provided the means by which we can take up the plow and fulfill our creational mandate. What are those means? Two things: (i) the gospel, and (ii) the power of the Spirit. The two are inseparable, for without the power of the Spirit, our efforts to cultivate creation into a godly civilization would be in vain. And without the gospel, we would have no context upon which to build such a civilization. The creational mandate is one of transformation, and transformation cannot occur without the two. But wait! Where did Jesus affirm the creational mandate? Where did Jesus reissue the mandate? Has not that mandate expired? No, it has not. There is not a single thread of thought in Scripture that suggests that it has. Instead, it has been renewed. Read carefully what Jesus commissioned the disciples to do in Matthew 28:18-20, a commission by the way which extends to *all* of God's people irregardless of the times:

> And Jesus came and said to them, "All authority in heaven and on earth has been given to me. Go therefore and make disciples of all nations, baptizing them in the name of the Father and of the Son and of the Holy Spirit, teaching them to observe all that I have commanded you. And behold, I am with you always, to the end of the age."

The creational mandate, or the *cultural* mandate, has been renewed in the Great Commission. Most followers of Jesus today, and I would add those at least of the past century, have not thought this far ahead. They have been taught a "myopic" gospel at best, a truncated gospel, which has as its *only* purpose to save man from his perdition and impending judgment. If we have saved a soul from eternal judgment, for example, and assured them a place in "heaven" when they die as a result of our missional efforts, then we have supposedly done enough. What they do from the moment of conversion on until the time of their deaths is of little importance, so long as they stay clear from sin. This interpretation (and application) of the Great Commission does a disservice to our Lord Jesus Christ and what He accomplished. Yes, Jesus died for our sins. Yes, Jesus secured for us eternal life in the hereafter. Yes, Jesus calls us to holy living. But there is *more* to the gospel than just saving and preserving us until we see Jesus. There is work to be done *now*. Our created purpose and call have been recovered in the Son. We have been redeemed in order that we might carry out the will of God. And what is the will of God? To make disciples of all the nations. And what happens when we successfully disciple the nations? We cultivate a godly civilization. It is an inevitable result. Consider that when the beliefs of a people change, their values change, their behaviours change, and then what results is that the culture changes. When the gospel begins to change hearts, a culture change is inevitable. But one of the reasons why we haven't witnessed this in the present, as notably as we have in past centuries, for example, is because the gospel we are preaching is incomplete, it has been truncated and turned into nothing more than a private individualized spiritualization. We need to renounce the cultural retreatist mentality that has caused us to commit such a disservice to the biblical gospel. We need to recover the biblical, all-encompassing scope of the gospel, understanding it within the context of the whole redemptive-historical narrative of Scripture. Believe it or not, this is one of the ways that Christ is bringing all things in subjection to Himself (1 Cor. 15:20-28), by means of the *renewed* creational mandate.

I liked what Voddie Baucham had to say on this when he spoke about work at the 2023 Founders Conference in Florida. He said that wherever God has placed us, *that* is our corner of the garden. And our mandate is to do whatever is in our power, by means of the proclamation and application of the gospel, to make that corner of the garden resemble as much as possible the Garden of Eden. It does not matter whether you are a plumber, a construction worker, a chemist, a politician, a legislator, whatever profession you have been given must be seen within the context of our call as God's vice-regents in Christ. It was the apostle Paul who wrote: "Whatever you do, work heartily, as for the Lord and not for men" (Col. 3:23), and, "So, whether you eat or drink, or whatever you do, do all to the glory of God" (1 Cor. 10:31). The Spirit of God will take care of the rest.

It should be increasingly clear to us, that the good news of the gospel is not just that Jesus has come as Saviour, but that He has also come as King. That famous line by the apostle Peter, "And there is salvation in no one else, for there is no other name under heaven given among men by which we must be saved" (Acts 4:12), was in fact first used by the Emperor Caesar Augustus concerning himself, and Peter knew well what it meant: Jesus is a saving King. He is the *King of kings*. His Kingship is *now* and it is all-encompassing. And as the King, He has *all* the power and *all* the authority to redeem *all of creation*, bringing all things subject to Himself (1 Cor. 15:28). In 1 Corinthians 15:24-28, Paul explains:

> Then comes the end, when he delivers the kingdom
> to God the Father after destroying every rule and
> every authority and power. For he must reign until
> he has put all his enemies under his feet. The last
> enemy to be destroyed is death. For "God has put
> all things in subjection under his feet." But when
> it says, "all things are put in subjection," it is plain
> that he is excepted who put all things in subjection
> under him. When all things are subjected to him,
> then the Son himself will also be subjected to him
> who put all things in subjection under him, that
> God may be all in all.

How will we know when our work is complete?
When, as a result of our fulfillment of the Great
Commission, all things (not necessarily *all people*,
but all of society) are brought subject to Christ.
We might call this the "triumph" of the gospel (Ps.
72; Isa. 2; Matt. 13:31-33; 24:14). And this will
include the inevitable defeat of God's enemies,
with that last enemy being "death." Yes, it is true
that Christ has given us new life. It is a new life
that we have now in the Spirit of God (Rom. 6:4;
2 Cor. 5:17; Eph. 4:22-24), but the full manifestation of that life that will take place when Jesus

returns (Matt. 24:27, 44; Heb. 9:28; Rev. 1:7). His return will mark the vanquishing of the reality of death once and for all, because it will be at that moment that He will raise His people who have fallen asleep (who have died, see 1 Thess. 4:14-15), and when He will consummate all things (2 Pet. 3:4-13; Rev. 21-22). That is our *biblical* anticipation, that Christ "comes soon" (Gr. μαρὰν ἀθά, *maranatha*) in order to bring to completion the redemption and renewal of creation, for our home is not high up in the heavens as many appear to believe, but here on earth (2 Pet. 3:13; Rev. 21:1). And in the meantime, what we do in the here and now *matters*, because we are building up the Kingdom of God. We are very much "kingdom builders" in Christ (Matt. 6:38), and that Kingdom will also be made fully manifest when our King, Jesus Christ, returns.

And when that time comes, we will then be given the new earth as our inheritance, for we are also joint heirs as adopted children of God (Rom. 8:16-17; Gal. 3:29; 1 Pet. 1:4). How the grace and goodness of God abounds! And guess what? Perhaps this is the real kicker: This will be no occasion to lay back and kick up your feet. There will be no lounging on luxurious loveseats while we have grapes fed to us by the angels. Many of the popular depictions of what the new earth will look like are unimaginative given their lack of footing in God's Word. The truth is: We will have work to do. Fulfilling work. Fruitful work. Kingdom-building work. God-glorifying work. What we do now is in preparation for what we will do then in service to our God and King. In the words of Baucham:

> Work is not a product of the fall. The arduous nature of our work is nature of the fall. Our laziness in the face of the work we have to do is a product of the fall... [But] work is not a product of the fall.[7]

The Hope that the Good News Brings

The prophet Isaiah, who prophesied of the Redeemer approximately 700 years prior, proclaimed under the inspiration of the Spirit of God:

> How beautiful upon the mountains are the feet of him who brings good news, who publishes peace, who brings good news of happiness, who publishes

---

7. Founders Ministries, "Work Isn't a Product of the Fall", *Youtube*. Accessed Feb. 1, 2023, https://www.youtube.com/watch?v=oW56EKecvFk/.

salvation, who says to Zion, "Your God reigns" (Isa. 52:7).

Why are the "feet" of this person called "beautiful"? Because he is running to us to deliver a message of "good news". What good news? The good news of Jesus, who has come as Saviour and King, the promised seed, the Redeemer of all creation. In Isaiah's time, it was a mystery that was yet to unfold, as it was for the rest of the Old Testament prophets; but for us it is a mystery revealed (1 Pet. 1:10). And now that we have this revelation, this "good news", how are we to respond? How are we to receive the good news of the messenger? First, we are to repent and believe in the One whom God has sent (Matt. 4:17; Acts 3:19; 17:30; Rom. 10:9). And secondly, we are to "proclaim [it] on the housetops" (Matt. 10:27). Yes, that means we are to share it with all those whom we know. The second springs forth from the first, because the gospel brings such joy that we cannot contain ourselves. And how could it not bring such joy? The gospel, the good news, after all, brings about peace and hope, it brings about healing and life, it brings about freedom and restoration. It brings about salvation and redemption.

And we first begin to see that in the heart of man before it spills out into all of what man does. And as time progresses, as God's people fulfill their purpose and call, we will see the Spirit of God bring to completion His redemptive plan at the appointed time. We all wait in anticipation for that day, when heaven and earth become one.

Take a moment and ponder the following: Can you imagine a world without sin? Can you imagine a world without sickness and disease? Can you imagine a world without evil and death? A world where there is perfect peace between man and God, between man and fellow man, and between man and creation. A world where man can function in perfect harmony with all the creational law spheres? It might seem like a fairytale, but it is so much more than that, it is our promised reality. And that biblical reality is most beautifully expressed by Scott James in his book *The Sower*, in which he states:

> Even now, the Sower calls out with wondrous power,
> and the world sings in return.
> The garden, once lost, is being remade.
> One day we will live with him there,

and as we listen to the sound of his Voice,
we will see him face to face.[8]

God has remedied (and is still at work remedying) what we have altered by our sin.

Glory be to God.

---

8. Scott James, *The Sower* (Wheaton, IL.: Crossway, 2022).

Chapter Five

CONCLUSION

WHAT THEN IS THE GOOD NEWS? What then is the gospel? Having now understood the *original* state of things. Having also understood what transpired to *alter* the state of things. And having understood what was done to *remedy* the state of things. The gospel can then be articulated as follows:

Creation

In the beginning, God created the heavens and the earth, and He called it "good." There was peace (*Shalom*) in every part of the earth as everything worked according to God's intention and design. There was peace between man and God, peace between man and fellow man, and peace between man and creation. The earth was created with human flourishment in mind, a place where man could live in the presence of God, fulfilling the creational mandate, and joyfully and lovingly worshipping the Creator.

Fall

Our first parents, Adam and Eve, whom were to be the prophets, priests, and designated king (and queen) of God, rejected God's rule in favour of their own radical autonomy, understood as (i) complete independence from God, and (ii) being a law unto oneself. We refer to this rebellious act as "the fall" because, as the head representatives of the human race, Adam and Eve's sin affects us too. Sin has caused a radical reversal in mankind; whereas before we were created originally upright, with true knowledge and in close communion with the living God, sin has ravaged our beings, marred our minds and image, and disrupted our communion with the divine by reorienting the direction of our worship towards that of creation, inevitably resulting in our total depravation, disorganization and decomposition.

Redemption

In response to our sin, the Creator God, who is perfectly just and thus determinedly wrathful toward sin, is just as determined to turn the evil and suffering which we have caused into good for His ultimate glory. The grand narrative of Scripture from Genesis to Revelation reveals God's plan for redeeming His creation and rescuing sinners from their fallen condition and impending judgment. Through the life, death and resurrection of Jesus Christ, God Himself has come to renew the world and restore His people. This work of renewal can be better understood as re-creation, beginning with the human heart and then extending to every creational aspect, until the day dawns when God's promise to renew all things comes into perfect fulfillment, with Christ returning to judge sin and evil once and for all and to usher in perfect righteousness and peace (*Shalom*) for all eternity.

This is the gospel, the *whole* gospel.

Scripture Index

ABOUT THE AUTHOR

STEVEN R. MARTINS is founding director of the Cántaro Institute and founding pastor of Sevilla Chapel in St. Catharines, ON. He has worked in the fields of missional apologetics and church leadership for over ten years and has spoken at numerous conferences, churches, and University student events. He has also contributed articles to *Coalición por el Evangelio* (TGC in Spanish) and the *Siglo XXI* journal of Editorial CLIR. Steven holds a Master's degree *summa cum laude* in Theological Studies with a focus on Christian apologetics from Veritas International University (Santa Ana, CA., USA) and a Bachelor of Human Resource Management from York University (Toronto, ON., Canada). Steven is married to Cindy and they live in Lincoln, Ontario, with their sons Matthias, Timothy, and Nehemías.

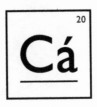

ABOUT THE CÁNTARO INSTITUTE

Inheriting, Informing, Inspiring

The Cántaro Institute is a reformed evangelical organization committed to the advancement of the Christian worldview for the reformation and renewal of the church and culture.

We believe that as the Christian church returns to the fount of Scripture as her ultimate authority for all knowing and living, and wisely applies God's truth to every aspect of life, her missiological activity will result in not only the renewal of the human person but also the reformation of culture, an inevitable result when the true scope and nature of the gospel is made known and applied.